Address Book

I. S. Anderson

Address Book

ISBN-10: 1523309563

ISBN-13: 978-1523309566

For more information regarding this publication, contact:
nahjpress@outlook.com

First Printing, 2016

Name: _____

Phone: _____

Cell: _____

Email: _____

Company: _____

Street: _____

City, State, Zip: _____

A

Name:	
Address:	
Home:	Cell:
Work:	Fax:
E-mail:	
Birthday:	
Notes:	

Name:	
Address:	
Home:	Cell:
Work:	Fax:
E-mail:	
Birthday:	
Notes:	

Name:	
Address:	
Home:	Cell:
Work:	Fax:
E-mail:	
Birthday:	
Notes:	

Name:	
Address:	
Home:	Cell:
Work:	Fax:
E-mail:	
Birthday:	
Notes:	

Name:	
Address:	
Home:	Cell:
Work:	Fax:
E-mail:	
Birthday:	
Notes:	

Name:	
Address:	
Home:	Cell:
Work:	Fax:
E-mail:	
Birthday:	
Notes:	

Name:

Address:

Home:	Cell:
Work:	Fax:

E-mail:

Birthday:

Notes:

Name:

Address:

Home:	Cell:
Work:	Fax:

E-mail:

Birthday:

Notes:

Name:

Address:

Home:	Cell:
Work:	Fax:

E-mail:

Birthday:

Notes:

Name:	
Address:	
Home:	Cell:
Work:	Fax:
E-mail:	
Birthday:	
Notes:	

Name:	
Address:	
Home:	Cell:
Work:	Fax:
E-mail:	
Birthday:	
Notes:	

Name:	
Address:	
Home:	Cell:
Work:	Fax:
E-mail:	
Birthday:	
Notes:	

A

Name:	
Address:	
Home:	Cell:
Work:	Fax:
E-mail:	
Birthday:	
Notes:	

Name:	
Address:	
Home:	Cell:
Work:	Fax:
E-mail:	
Birthday:	
Notes:	

Name:	
Address:	
Home:	Cell:
Work:	Fax:
E-mail:	
Birthday:	
Notes:	

A

Name:

Address:

Home:	Cell:
Work:	Fax:

E-mail:

Birthday:

Notes:

Name:

Address:

Home:	Cell:
Work:	Fax:

E-mail:

Birthday:

Notes:

Name:

Address:

Home:	Cell:
Work:	Fax:

E-mail:

Birthday:

Notes:

Name:	
Address:	
Home:	Cell:
Work:	Fax:
E-mail:	
Birthday:	
Notes:	

Name:	
Address:	
Home:	Cell:
Work:	Fax:
E-mail:	
Birthday:	
Notes:	

Name:	
Address:	
Home:	Cell:
Work:	Fax:
E-mail:	
Birthday:	
Notes:	

Name:

Address:

Home: | Cell:

Work: | Fax:

E-mail:

Birthday:

Notes:

Name:

Address:

Home: | Cell:

Work: | Fax:

E-mail:

Birthday:

Notes:

Name:

Address:

Home: | Cell:

Work: | Fax:

E-mail:

Birthday:

Notes:

Name:

Address:

Home: Cell:

Work: Fax:

E-mail:

Birthday:

Notes:

Name:

Address:

Home: Cell:

Work: Fax:

E-mail:

Birthday:

Notes:

Name:

Address:

Home: Cell:

Work: Fax:

E-mail:

Birthday:

Notes:

Name:

Address:	
Home:	Cell:
Work:	Fax:
E-mail:	
Birthday:	
Notes:	

Name:

Address:	
Home:	Cell:
Work:	Fax:
E-mail:	
Birthday:	
Notes:	

Name:

Address:	
Home:	Cell:
Work:	Fax:
E-mail:	
Birthday:	
Notes:	

Name:	
Address:	
Home:	Cell:
Work:	Fax:
E-mail:	
Birthday:	
Notes:	

Name:	
Address:	
Home:	Cell:
Work:	Fax:
E-mail:	
Birthday:	
Notes:	

Name:	
Address:	
Home:	Cell:
Work:	Fax:
E-mail:	
Birthday:	
Notes:	

B

Name:	
Address:	
Home:	Cell:
Work:	Fax:
E-mail:	
Birthday:	
Notes:	

Name:	
Address:	
Home:	Cell:
Work:	Fax:
E-mail:	
Birthday:	
Notes:	

Name:	
Address:	
Home:	Cell:
Work:	Fax:
E-mail:	
Birthday:	
Notes:	

C

Name:	
Address:	
Home:	Cell:
Work:	Fax:
E-mail:	
Birthday:	
Notes:	

Name:	
Address:	
Home:	Cell:
Work:	Fax:
E-mail:	
Birthday:	
Notes:	

Name:	
Address:	
Home:	Cell:
Work:	Fax:
E-mail:	
Birthday:	
Notes:	

Name:

Address:	
Home:	Cell:
Work:	Fax:
E-mail:	
Birthday:	
Notes:	

Name:

Address:	
Home:	Cell:
Work:	Fax:
E-mail:	
Birthday:	
Notes:	

Name:

Address:	
Home:	Cell:
Work:	Fax:
E-mail:	
Birthday:	
Notes:	

Name:	
Address:	
Home:	Cell:
Work:	Fax:
E-mail:	
Birthday:	
Notes:	

Name:	
Address:	
Home:	Cell:
Work:	Fax:
E-mail:	
Birthday:	
Notes:	

Name:	
Address:	
Home:	Cell:
Work:	Fax:
E-mail:	
Birthday:	
Notes:	

Name:

Address:

Home: Cell:

Work: Fax:

E-mail:

Birthday:

Notes:

Name:

Address:

Home: Cell:

Work: Fax:

E-mail:

Birthday:

Notes:

Name:

Address:

Home: Cell:

Work: Fax:

E-mail:

Birthday:

Notes:

C

Name:

Address:

Home:	Cell:
Work:	Fax:

E-mail:
Birthday:
Notes:

Name:

Address:

Home:	Cell:
Work:	Fax:

E-mail:
Birthday:
Notes:

Name:

Address:

Home:	Cell:
Work:	Fax:

E-mail:
Birthday:
Notes:

Name:

Address:

Home: Cell:

Work: Fax:

E-mail:

Birthday:

Notes:

Name:

Address:

Home: Cell:

Work: Fax:

E-mail:

Birthday:

Notes:

Name:

Address:

Home: Cell:

Work: Fax:

E-mail:

Birthday:

Notes:

D

Name:	
Address:	
Home:	Cell:
Work:	Fax:
E-mail:	
Birthday:	
Notes:	

Name:	
Address:	
Home:	Cell:
Work:	Fax:
E-mail:	
Birthday:	
Notes:	

Name:	
Address:	
Home:	Cell:
Work:	Fax:
E-mail:	
Birthday:	
Notes:	

Name:

Address:

Home: Cell:

Work: Fax:

E-mail:

Birthday:

Notes:

Name:

Address:

Home: Cell:

Work: Fax:

E-mail:

Birthday:

Notes:

Name:

Address:

Home: Cell:

Work: Fax:

E-mail:

Birthday:

Notes:

Name:

Address:

Home: Cell:

Work: Fax:

E-mail:

Birthday:

Notes:

Name:

Address:

Home: Cell:

Work: Fax:

E-mail:

Birthday:

Notes:

Name:

Address:

Home: Cell:

Work: Fax:

E-mail:

Birthday:

Notes:

Name:	
Address:	
Home:	Cell:
Work:	Fax:
E-mail:	
Birthday:	
Notes:	

Name:	
Address:	
Home:	Cell:
Work:	Fax:
E-mail:	
Birthday:	
Notes:	

Name:	
Address:	
Home:	Cell:
Work:	Fax:
E-mail:	
Birthday:	
Notes:	

D

Name:	
Address:	
Home:	Cell:
Work:	Fax:
E-mail:	
Birthday:	
Notes:	

Name:	
Address:	
Home:	Cell:
Work:	Fax:
E-mail:	
Birthday:	
Notes:	

Name:	
Address:	
Home:	Cell:
Work:	Fax:
E-mail:	
Birthday:	
Notes:	

Name:

Address:

Home: Cell:

Work: Fax:

E-mail:

Birthday:

Notes:

Name:

Address:

Home: Cell:

Work: Fax:

E-mail:

Birthday:

Notes:

Name:

Address:

Home: Cell:

Work: Fax:

E-mail:

Birthday:

Notes:

Name:

Address:

Home: Cell:

Work: Fax:

E-mail:

Birthday:

Notes:

Name:

Address:

Home: Cell:

Work: Fax:

E-mail:

Birthday:

Notes:

Name:

Address:

Home: Cell:

Work: Fax:

E-mail:

Birthday:

Notes:

Name:

Address:	
Home:	Cell:
Work:	Fax:
E-mail:	
Birthday:	
Notes:	

Name:

Address:	
Home:	Cell:
Work:	Fax:
E-mail:	
Birthday:	
Notes:	

Name:

Address:	
Home:	Cell:
Work:	Fax:
E-mail:	
Birthday:	
Notes:	

Name:

Address:	
Home:	Cell:
Work:	Fax:
E-mail:	
Birthday:	
Notes:	

Name:

Address:	
Home:	Cell:
Work:	Fax:
E-mail:	
Birthday:	
Notes:	

Name:

Address:	
Home:	Cell:
Work:	Fax:
E-mail:	
Birthday:	
Notes:	

Name:

Address:

Home:	Cell:
Work:	Fax:

E-mail:

Birthday:

Notes:

Name:

Address:

Home:	Cell:
Work:	Fax:

E-mail:

Birthday:

Notes:

Name:

Address:

Home:	Cell:
Work:	Fax:

E-mail:

Birthday:

Notes:

Name:	
Address:	
Home:	Cell:
Work:	Fax:
E-mail:	
Birthday:	
Notes:	

Name:	
Address:	
Home:	Cell:
Work:	Fax:
E-mail:	
Birthday:	
Notes:	

Name:	
Address:	
Home:	Cell:
Work:	Fax:
E-mail:	
Birthday:	
Notes:	

Name:

Address:

Home: Cell:

Work: Fax:

E-mail:

Birthday:

Notes:

Name:

Address:

Home: Cell:

Work: Fax:

E-mail:

Birthday:

Notes:

Name:

Address:

Home: Cell:

Work: Fax:

E-mail:

Birthday:

Notes:

Name:	
Address:	
Home:	Cell:
Work:	Fax:
E-mail:	
Birthday:	
Notes:	

Name:	
Address:	
Home:	Cell:
Work:	Fax:
E-mail:	
Birthday:	
Notes:	

Name:	
Address:	
Home:	Cell:
Work:	Fax:
E-mail:	
Birthday:	
Notes:	

Name:

Address:

Home:	Cell:
Work:	Fax:

E-mail:

Birthday:

Notes:

Name:

Address:

Home:	Cell:
Work:	Fax:

E-mail:

Birthday:

Notes:

Name:

Address:

Home:	Cell:
Work:	Fax:

E-mail:

Birthday:

Notes:

Name:

Address:

Home: Cell:

Work: Fax:

E-mail:

Birthday:

Notes:

Name:

Address:

Home: Cell:

Work: Fax:

E-mail:

Birthday:

Notes:

Name:

Address:

Home: Cell:

Work: Fax:

E-mail:

Birthday:

Notes:

Name:

Address:

Home: Cell:

Work: Fax:

E-mail:

Birthday:

Notes:

Name:

Address:

Home: Cell:

Work: Fax:

E-mail:

Birthday:

Notes:

Name:

Address:

Home: Cell:

Work: Fax:

E-mail:

Birthday:

Notes:

Name:

Address:

Home:	Cell:
Work:	Fax:

E-mail:

Birthday:

Notes:

F

Name:

Address:

Home:	Cell:
Work:	Fax:

E-mail:

Birthday:

Notes:

Name:

Address:

Home:	Cell:
Work:	Fax:

E-mail:

Birthday:

Notes:

Name:

Address:

Home: Cell:

Work: Fax:

E-mail:

Birthday:

Notes:

Name:

Address:

Home: Cell:

Work: Fax:

E-mail:

Birthday:

Notes:

Name:

Address:

Home: Cell:

Work: Fax:

E-mail:

Birthday:

Notes:

Name:

Address:

Home: Cell:

Work: Fax:

E-mail:

Birthday:

Notes:

G

Name:

Address:

Home: Cell:

Work: Fax:

E-mail:

Birthday:

Notes:

Name:

Address:

Home: Cell:

Work: Fax:

E-mail:

Birthday:

Notes:

Name:	
Address:	
Home:	Cell:
Work:	Fax:
E-mail:	
Birthday:	
Notes:	

Name:	
Address:	
Home:	Cell:
Work:	Fax:
E-mail:	
Birthday:	
Notes:	

Name:	
Address:	
Home:	Cell:
Work:	Fax:
E-mail:	
Birthday:	
Notes:	

Name:

Address:

Home: Cell:

Work: Fax:

E-mail:

Birthday:

Notes:

Name:

Address:

Home: Cell:

Work: Fax:

E-mail:

Birthday:

Notes:

Name:

Address:

Home: Cell:

Work: Fax:

E-mail:

Birthday:

Notes:

Name:

Address:

Home: Cell:

Work: Fax:

E-mail:

Birthday:

Notes:

G

Name:

Address:

Home: Cell:

Work: Fax:

E-mail:

Birthday:

Notes:

Name:

Address:

Home: Cell:

Work: Fax:

E-mail:

Birthday:

Notes:

Name:

Address:

Home: Cell:

Work: Fax:

E-mail:

Birthday:

Notes:

G

Name:

Address:

Home: Cell:

Work: Fax:

E-mail:

Birthday:

Notes:

Name:

Address:

Home: Cell:

Work: Fax:

E-mail:

Birthday:

Notes:

Name:	
Address:	
Home:	Cell:
Work:	Fax:
E-mail:	
Birthday:	
Notes:	

G

Name:	
Address:	
Home:	Cell:
Work:	Fax:
E-mail:	
Birthday:	
Notes:	

Name:	
Address:	
Home:	Cell:
Work:	Fax:
E-mail:	
Birthday:	
Notes:	

Name:

Address:

Home:	Cell:
Work:	Fax:

E-mail:

Birthday:

Notes:

H

Name:

Address:

Home:	Cell:
Work:	Fax:

E-mail:

Birthday:

Notes:

Name:

Address:

Home:	Cell:
Work:	Fax:

E-mail:

Birthday:

Notes:

Name:

Address:

Home: Cell:

Work: Fax:

E-mail:

Birthday:

Notes:

Name:

Address:

Home: Cell:

Work: Fax:

E-mail:

Birthday:

Notes:

Name:

Address:

Home: Cell:

Work: Fax:

E-mail:

Birthday:

Notes:

Name:

Address:

Home: Cell:

Work: Fax:

E-mail:

Birthday:

Notes:

Name:

Address:

Home: Cell:

Work: Fax:

E-mail:

Birthday:

Notes:

Name:

Address:

Home: Cell:

Work: Fax:

E-mail:

Birthday:

Notes:

H

Name:

Address:

Home:	Cell:
Work:	Fax:

E-mail:

Birthday:

Notes:

Name:

Address:

Home:	Cell:
Work:	Fax:

E-mail:

Birthday:

Notes:

Name:

Address:

Home:	Cell:
Work:	Fax:

E-mail:

Birthday:

Notes:

Name:	
Address:	
Home:	Cell:
Work:	Fax:
E-mail:	
Birthday:	
Notes:	

Name:	
Address:	
Home:	Cell:
Work:	Fax:
E-mail:	
Birthday:	
Notes:	

Name:	
Address:	
Home:	Cell:
Work:	Fax:
E-mail:	
Birthday:	
Notes:	

Name:	
Address:	
Home:	Cell:
Work:	Fax:
E-mail:	
Birthday:	
Notes:	

H

Name:	
Address:	
Home:	Cell:
Work:	Fax:
E-mail:	
Birthday:	
Notes:	

Name:	
Address:	
Home:	Cell:
Work:	Fax:
E-mail:	
Birthday:	
Notes:	

Name:	
Address:	
Home:	Cell:
Work:	Fax:
E-mail:	
Birthday:	
Notes:	

Name:	
Address:	
Home:	Cell:
Work:	Fax:
E-mail:	
Birthday:	
Notes:	

Name:	
Address:	
Home:	Cell:
Work:	Fax:
E-mail:	
Birthday:	
Notes:	

Name:	
Address:	
Home:	Cell:
Work:	Fax:
E-mail:	
Birthday:	
Notes:	

Name:	
Address:	
Home:	Cell:
Work:	Fax:
E-mail:	
Birthday:	
Notes:	

Name:	
Address:	
Home:	Cell:
Work:	Fax:
E-mail:	
Birthday:	
Notes:	

Name:

Address:

Home: Cell:

Work: Fax:

E-mail:

Birthday:

Notes:

I

Name:

Address:

Home: Cell:

Work: Fax:

E-mail:

Birthday:

Notes:

Name:

Address:

Home: Cell:

Work: Fax:

E-mail:

Birthday:

Notes:

Name:

Address:

Home: Cell:

Work: Fax:

E-mail:

Birthday:

Notes:

Name:

Address:

Home: Cell:

Work: Fax:

E-mail:

Birthday:

Notes:

Name:

Address:

Home: Cell:

Work: Fax:

E-mail:

Birthday:

Notes:

Name:

Address:

Home:	Cell:
Work:	Fax:

E-mail:

Birthday:

Notes:

Name:

Address:

Home:	Cell:
Work:	Fax:

E-mail:

Birthday:

Notes:

Name:

Address:

Home:	Cell:
Work:	Fax:

E-mail:

Birthday:

Notes:

I

Name:

Address:

Home: Cell:

Work: Fax:

E-mail:

Birthday:

Notes:

Name:

Address:

Home: Cell:

Work: Fax:

E-mail:

Birthday:

Notes:

Name:

Address:

Home: Cell:

Work: Fax:

E-mail:

Birthday:

Notes:

Name:

Address:

Home: Cell:

Work: Fax:

E-mail:

Birthday:

Notes:

Name:

Address:

Home: Cell:

Work: Fax:

E-mail:

Birthday:

Notes:

Name:

Address:

Home: Cell:

Work: Fax:

E-mail:

Birthday:

Notes:

Name:

Address:	
Home:	Cell:
Work:	Fax:
E-mail:	
Birthday:	
Notes:	

Name:

Address:	
Home:	Cell:
Work:	Fax:
E-mail:	
Birthday:	
Notes:	

Name:

Address:	
Home:	Cell:
Work:	Fax:
E-mail:	
Birthday:	
Notes:	

Name:

Address:

Home: Cell:

Work: Fax:

E-mail:

Birthday:

Notes:

Name:

Address:

Home: Cell:

Work: Fax:

E-mail:

Birthday:

Notes:

Name:

Address:

Home: Cell:

Work: Fax:

E-mail:

Birthday:

Notes:

Name:	
Address:	
Home:	Cell:
Work:	Fax:
E-mail:	
Birthday:	
Notes:	

Name:	
Address:	
Home:	Cell:
Work:	Fax:
E-mail:	
Birthday:	
Notes:	

Name:	
Address:	
Home:	Cell:
Work:	Fax:
E-mail:	
Birthday:	
Notes:	

Name:	
Address:	
Home:	Cell:
Work:	Fax:
E-mail:	
Birthday:	
Notes:	

Name:	
Address:	
Home:	Cell:
Work:	Fax:
E-mail:	
Birthday:	
Notes:	

Name:	
Address:	
Home:	Cell:
Work:	Fax:
E-mail:	
Birthday:	
Notes:	

Name:

Address:

Home:	Cell:
Work:	Fax:

E-mail:

Birthday:

Notes:

Name:

Address:

Home:	Cell:
Work:	Fax:

E-mail:

Birthday:

Notes:

Name:

Address:

Home:	Cell:
Work:	Fax:

E-mail:

Birthday:

Notes:

Name:

Address:

Home:	Cell:
Work:	Fax:

E-mail:

Birthday:

Notes:

Name:

Address:

Home:	Cell:
Work:	Fax:

E-mail:

Birthday:

Notes:

Name:

Address:

Home:	Cell:
Work:	Fax:

E-mail:

Birthday:

Notes:

Name:

Address:

Home: Cell:

Work: Fax:

E-mail:

Birthday:

Notes:

Name:

Address:

Home: Cell:

Work: Fax:

E-mail:

Birthday:

Notes:

Name:

Address:

Home: Cell:

Work: Fax:

E-mail:

Birthday:

Notes:

Name:

Address:

Home: Cell:

Work: Fax:

E-mail:

Birthday:

Notes:

K **Name:**

Address:

Home: Cell:

Work: Fax:

E-mail:

Birthday:

Notes:

Name:

Address:

Home: Cell:

Work: Fax:

E-mail:

Birthday:

Notes:

Name:

Address:	
Home:	Cell:
Work:	Fax:
E-mail:	
Birthday:	
Notes:	

Name:

Address:	
Home:	Cell:
Work:	Fax:
E-mail:	
Birthday:	
Notes:	

Name:

Address:	
Home:	Cell:
Work:	Fax:
E-mail:	
Birthday:	
Notes:	

Name:

Address:

Home: Cell:

Work: Fax:

E-mail:

Birthday:

Notes:

Name:

Address:

Home: Cell:

Work: Fax:

E-mail:

Birthday:

Notes:

Name:

Address:

Home: Cell:

Work: Fax:

E-mail:

Birthday:

Notes:

Name:

Address:

Home: Cell:

Work: Fax:

E-mail:

Birthday:

Notes:

Name:

Address:

Home: Cell:

Work: Fax:

E-mail:

Birthday:

Notes:

Name:

Address:

Home: Cell:

Work: Fax:

E-mail:

Birthday:

Notes:

Name:

Address:

Home: | Cell:

Work: | Fax:

E-mail:

Birthday:

Notes:

L

Name:

Address:

Home: | Cell:

Work: | Fax:

E-mail:

Birthday:

Notes:

Name:

Address:

Home: | Cell:

Work: | Fax:

E-mail:

Birthday:

Notes:

Name:

Address:

Home: Cell:

Work: Fax:

E-mail:

Birthday:

Notes:

Name:

Address:

Home: Cell:

Work: Fax:

E-mail:

Birthday:

Notes:

Name:

Address:

Home: Cell:

Work: Fax:

E-mail:

Birthday:

Notes:

Name:

Address:	
Home:	Cell:
Work:	Fax:
E-mail:	
Birthday:	
Notes:	

Name:

L

Address:	
Home:	Cell:
Work:	Fax:
E-mail:	
Birthday:	
Notes:	

Name:

Address:	
Home:	Cell:
Work:	Fax:
E-mail:	
Birthday:	
Notes:	

Name:	
Address:	
Home:	Cell:
Work:	Fax:
E-mail:	
Birthday:	
Notes:	

Name:	
Address:	
Home:	Cell:
Work:	Fax:
E-mail:	
Birthday:	
Notes:	

L

Name:	
Address:	
Home:	Cell:
Work:	Fax:
E-mail:	
Birthday:	
Notes:	

Name:

Address:

Home: Cell:

Work: Fax:

E-mail:

Birthday:

Notes:

Name:

Address:

Home: Cell:

Work: Fax:

E-mail:

Birthday:

Notes:

Name:

Address:

Home: Cell:

Work: Fax:

E-mail:

Birthday:

Notes:

L

Name:

Address:	
Home:	Cell:
Work:	Fax:
E-mail:	
Birthday:	
Notes:	

Name:

Address:	
Home:	Cell:
Work:	Fax:
E-mail:	
Birthday:	
Notes:	

Name:

Address:	
Home:	Cell:
Work:	Fax:
E-mail:	
Birthday:	
Notes:	

Name:

Address:

Home: Cell:

Work: Fax:

E-mail:

Birthday:

Notes:

Name:

Address:

M

Home: Cell:

Work: Fax:

E-mail:

Birthday:

Notes:

Name:

Address:

Home: Cell:

Work: Fax:

E-mail:

Birthday:

Notes:

Name:

Address:

Home:	Cell:
Work:	Fax:

E-mail:

Birthday:

Notes:

Name:

Address:

Home:	Cell:
Work:	Fax:

E-mail:

Birthday:

Notes:

Name:

Address:

Home:	Cell:
Work:	Fax:

E-mail:

Birthday:

Notes:

Name:	
Address:	
Home:	Cell:
Work:	Fax:
E-mail:	
Birthday:	
Notes:	

Name:	
Address:	
Home:	Cell:
Work:	Fax:
E-mail:	
Birthday:	
Notes:	

Name:	
Address:	
Home:	Cell:
Work:	Fax:
E-mail:	
Birthday:	
Notes:	

Name:	
Address:	
Home:	Cell:
Work:	Fax:
E-mail:	
Birthday:	
Notes:	

M

Name:	
Address:	
Home:	Cell:
Work:	Fax:
E-mail:	
Birthday:	
Notes:	

Name:	
Address:	
Home:	Cell:
Work:	Fax:
E-mail:	
Birthday:	
Notes:	

Name:

Address:

Home:	Cell:
Work:	Fax:

E-mail:

Birthday:

Notes:

Name:

Address:

Home:	Cell:
Work:	Fax:

E-mail:

Birthday:

Notes:

Name:

Address:

Home:	Cell:
Work:	Fax:

E-mail:

Birthday:

Notes:

Name:	
Address:	
Home:	Cell:
Work:	Fax:
E-mail:	
Birthday:	
Notes:	

Name:	
Address:	
Home:	Cell:
Work:	Fax:
E-mail:	
Birthday:	
Notes:	

Name:	
Address:	
Home:	Cell:
Work:	Fax:
E-mail:	
Birthday:	
Notes:	

Name:

Address:

Home:	Cell:
Work:	Fax:

E-mail:

Birthday:

Notes:

Name:

Address:

Home:	Cell:
Work:	Fax:

E-mail:

Birthday:

Notes:

Name:

Address:

Home:	Cell:
Work:	Fax:

E-mail:

Birthday:

Notes:

Name:

Address:

Home: Cell:

Work: Fax:

E-mail:

Birthday:

Notes:

Name:

Address:

Home: Cell:

Work: Fax:

E-mail:

Birthday:

Notes:

Name:

Address:

Home: Cell:

Work: Fax:

E-mail:

Birthday:

Notes:

Name:

Address:

Home: Cell:

Work: Fax:

E-mail:

Birthday:

Notes:

Name:

Address:

Home: Cell:

Work: Fax:

E-mail:

Birthday:

Notes:

Name:

Address:

Home: Cell:

Work: Fax:

E-mail:

Birthday:

Notes:

Name:

Address:

Home:	Cell:
Work:	Fax:

E-mail:

Birthday:

Notes:

Name:

Address:

Home:	Cell:
Work:	Fax:

E-mail:

Birthday:

Notes:

Name:

Address:

Home:	Cell:
Work:	Fax:

E-mail:

Birthday:

Notes:

Name:	
Address:	
Home:	Cell:
Work:	Fax:
E-mail:	
Birthday:	
Notes:	

Name:	
Address:	
Home:	Cell:
Work:	Fax:
E-mail:	
Birthday:	
Notes:	

Name:	
Address:	
Home:	Cell:
Work:	Fax:
E-mail:	
Birthday:	
Notes:	

Name:	
Address:	
Home:	Cell:
Work:	Fax:
E-mail:	
Birthday:	
Notes:	

Name:	
Address:	
Home:	Cell:
Work:	Fax:
E-mail:	
Birthday:	
Notes:	

Name:	
Address:	
Home:	Cell:
Work:	Fax:
E-mail:	
Birthday:	
Notes:	

Name:

Address:

Home: | Cell:

Work: | Fax:

E-mail:

Birthday:

Notes:

Name:

Address:

Home: | Cell:

Work: | Fax:

E-mail:

Birthday:

Notes:

Name:

Address:

Home: | Cell:

Work: | Fax:

E-mail:

Birthday:

Notes:

O

Name:

Address:	
Home:	Cell:
Work:	Fax:
E-mail:	
Birthday:	
Notes:	

Name:

Address:	
Home:	Cell:
Work:	Fax:
E-mail:	
Birthday:	
Notes:	

O

Name:

Address:	
Home:	Cell:
Work:	Fax:
E-mail:	
Birthday:	
Notes:	

Name:

Address:

Home: Cell:

Work: Fax:

E-mail:

Birthday:

Notes:

Name:

Address:

Home: Cell:

Work: Fax:

E-mail:

Birthday:

Notes:

Name:

Address:

Home: Cell:

Work: Fax:

E-mail:

Birthday:

Notes:

Name:	
Address:	
Home:	Cell:
Work:	Fax:
E-mail:	
Birthday:	
Notes:	

Name:	
Address:	
Home:	Cell:
Work:	Fax:
E-mail:	
Birthday:	
Notes:	

Name:	
Address:	
Home:	Cell:
Work:	Fax:
E-mail:	
Birthday:	
Notes:	

Name:

Address:

Home: Cell:

Work: Fax:

E-mail:

Birthday:

Notes:

Name:

Address:

Home: Cell:

Work: Fax:

E-mail:

Birthday:

Notes:

Name:

Address:

Home: Cell:

Work: Fax:

E-mail:

Birthday:

Notes:

Name:	
Address:	
Home:	Cell:
Work:	Fax:
E-mail:	
Birthday:	
Notes:	

Name:	
Address:	
Home:	Cell:
Work:	Fax:
E-mail:	
Birthday:	
Notes:	

O

Name:	
Address:	
Home:	Cell:
Work:	Fax:
E-mail:	
Birthday:	
Notes:	

Name:

Address:

Home: Cell:

Work: Fax:

E-mail:

Birthday:

Notes:

Name:

Address:

Home: Cell:

Work: Fax:

E-mail:

Birthday:

Notes:

Name:

Address:

Home: Cell:

Work: Fax:

E-mail:

Birthday:

Notes:

Name:

Address:

Home: Cell:

Work: Fax:

E-mail:

Birthday:

Notes:

Name:

Address:

Home: Cell:

Work: Fax:

E-mail:

Birthday:

Notes:

Name:

Address:

Home: Cell:

Work: Fax:

E-mail:

Birthday:

Notes:

Name:

Address:

Home: Cell:

Work: Fax:

E-mail:

Birthday:

Notes:

Name:

Address:

Home: Cell:

Work: Fax:

E-mail:

Birthday:

Notes:

Name:

Address:

Home: Cell:

Work: Fax:

E-mail:

Birthday:

Notes:

Name:	
Address:	
Home:	Cell:
Work:	Fax:
E-mail:	
Birthday:	
Notes:	

Name:	
Address:	
Home:	Cell:
Work:	Fax:
E-mail:	
Birthday:	
Notes:	

P

Name:	
Address:	
Home:	Cell:
Work:	Fax:
E-mail:	
Birthday:	
Notes:	

Name:	
Address:	
Home:	Cell:
Work:	Fax:
E-mail:	
Birthday:	
Notes:	

Name:	
Address:	
Home:	Cell:
Work:	Fax:
E-mail:	
Birthday:	
Notes:	

Name:	
Address:	
Home:	Cell:
Work:	Fax:
E-mail:	
Birthday:	
Notes:	

Name:

Address:

Home:	Cell:
Work:	Fax:

E-mail:

Birthday:

Notes:

Name:

Address:

Home:	Cell:
Work:	Fax:

E-mail:

Birthday:

Notes:

P

Name:

Address:

Home:	Cell:
Work:	Fax:

E-mail:

Birthday:

Notes:

Name:	
Address:	
Home:	Cell:
Work:	Fax:
E-mail:	
Birthday:	
Notes:	

Name:	
Address:	
Home:	Cell:
Work:	Fax:
E-mail:	
Birthday:	
Notes:	

Q

Name:	
Address:	
Home:	Cell:
Work:	Fax:
E-mail:	
Birthday:	
Notes:	

Name:

Address:

Home: Cell:

Work: Fax:

E-mail:

Birthday:

Notes:

Name:

Address:

Home: Cell:

Work: Fax:

E-mail:

Birthday:

Notes:

Name:

Address:

Home: Cell:

Work: Fax:

E-mail:

Birthday:

Notes:

Name:	
Address:	
Home:	Cell:
Work:	Fax:
E-mail:	
Birthday:	
Notes:	

Name:	
Address:	
Home:	Cell:
Work:	Fax:
E-mail:	
Birthday:	
Notes:	

Name:	
Address:	
Home:	Cell:
Work:	Fax:
E-mail:	
Birthday:	
Notes:	

Name:	
Address:	
Home:	Cell:
Work:	Fax:
E-mail:	
Birthday:	
Notes:	

Name:	
Address:	
Home:	Cell:
Work:	Fax:
E-mail:	
Birthday:	
Notes:	

Q

Name:	
Address:	
Home:	Cell:
Work:	Fax:
E-mail:	
Birthday:	
Notes:	

Name:	
Address:	
Home:	Cell:
Work:	Fax:
E-mail:	
Birthday:	
Notes:	

Name:	
Address:	
Home:	Cell:
Work:	Fax:
E-mail:	
Birthday:	
Notes:	

Name:	
Address:	
Home:	Cell:
Work:	Fax:
E-mail:	
Birthday:	
Notes:	

Name:	
Address:	
Home:	Cell:
Work:	Fax:
E-mail:	
Birthday:	
Notes:	

Name:	
Address:	
Home:	Cell:
Work:	Fax:
E-mail:	
Birthday:	
Notes:	

Q

Name:	
Address:	
Home:	Cell:
Work:	Fax:
E-mail:	
Birthday:	
Notes:	

Name:	
Address:	
Home:	Cell:
Work:	Fax:
E-mail:	
Birthday:	
Notes:	

Name:	
Address:	
Home:	Cell:
Work:	Fax:
E-mail:	
Birthday:	
Notes:	

R

Name:	
Address:	
Home:	Cell:
Work:	Fax:
E-mail:	
Birthday:	
Notes:	

Name:

Address:

Home: Cell:

Work: Fax:

E-mail:

Birthday:

Notes:

Name:

Address:

Home: Cell:

Work: Fax:

E-mail:

Birthday:

Notes:

Name:

Address:

Home: Cell:

Work: Fax:

E-mail:

Birthday:

Notes:

Name:

Address:

Home: Cell:

Work: Fax:

E-mail:

Birthday:

Notes:

Name:

Address:

Home: Cell:

Work: Fax:

E-mail:

Birthday:

Notes:

Name:

Address:

Home: Cell:

Work: Fax:

E-mail:

Birthday:

Notes:

Name:

Address:

Home: Cell:

Work: Fax:

E-mail:

Birthday:

Notes:

Name:

Address:

Home: Cell:

Work: Fax:

E-mail:

Birthday:

Notes:

Name:

Address:

Home: Cell:

Work: Fax:

E-mail:

Birthday:

Notes:

Name:

Address:

Home: Cell:

Work: Fax:

E-mail:

Birthday:

Notes:

Name:

Address:

Home: Cell:

Work: Fax:

E-mail:

Birthday:

Notes:

R

Name:

Address:

Home: Cell:

Work: Fax:

E-mail:

Birthday:

Notes:

Name:

Address:	
Home:	Cell:
Work:	Fax:
E-mail:	
Birthday:	
Notes:	

Name:

Address:	
Home:	Cell:
Work:	Fax:
E-mail:	
Birthday:	
Notes:	

Name:

Address:	
Home:	Cell:
Work:	Fax:
E-mail:	
Birthday:	
Notes:	

R

Name:	
Address:	
Home:	Cell:
Work:	Fax:
E-mail:	
Birthday:	
Notes:	

Name:	
Address:	
Home:	Cell:
Work:	Fax:
E-mail:	
Birthday:	
Notes:	

S

Name:	
Address:	
Home:	Cell:
Work:	Fax:
E-mail:	
Birthday:	
Notes:	

Name:

Address:

Home:	Cell:
Work:	Fax:

E-mail:

Birthday:

Notes:

Name:

Address:

Home:	Cell:
Work:	Fax:

E-mail:

Birthday:

Notes:

Name:

Address:

Home:	Cell:
Work:	Fax:

E-mail:

Birthday:

Notes:

Name:

Address:

Home: Cell:

Work: Fax:

E-mail:

Birthday:

Notes:

Name:

Address:

Home: Cell:

Work: Fax:

E-mail:

Birthday:

Notes:

S

Name:

Address:

Home: Cell:

Work: Fax:

E-mail:

Birthday:

Notes:

Name:	
Address:	
Home:	Cell:
Work:	Fax:
E-mail:	
Birthday:	
Notes:	

Name:	
Address:	
Home:	Cell:
Work:	Fax:
E-mail:	
Birthday:	
Notes:	

S

Name:	
Address:	
Home:	Cell:
Work:	Fax:
E-mail:	
Birthday:	
Notes:	

Name:	
Address:	
Home:	Cell:
Work:	Fax:
E-mail:	
Birthday:	
Notes:	

Name:	
Address:	
Home:	Cell:
Work:	Fax:
E-mail:	
Birthday:	
Notes:	

S

Name:	
Address:	
Home:	Cell:
Work:	Fax:
E-mail:	
Birthday:	
Notes:	

Name:	
Address:	
Home:	Cell:
Work:	Fax:
E-mail:	
Birthday:	
Notes:	

Name:	
Address:	
Home:	Cell:
Work:	Fax:
E-mail:	
Birthday:	
Notes:	

S

Name:	
Address:	
Home:	Cell:
Work:	Fax:
E-mail:	
Birthday:	
Notes:	

Name:

Address:

Home: Cell:

Work: Fax:

E-mail:

Birthday:

Notes:

Name:

Address:

Home: Cell:

Work: Fax:

E-mail:

Birthday:

Notes:

T

Name:

Address:

Home: Cell:

Work: Fax:

E-mail:

Birthday:

Notes:

Name:

Address:

Home: Cell:

Work: Fax:

E-mail:

Birthday:

Notes:

Name:

Address:

Home: Cell:

Work: Fax:

E-mail:

Birthday:

Notes:

T

Name:

Address:

Home: Cell:

Work: Fax:

E-mail:

Birthday:

Notes:

Name:

Address:	
Home:	Cell:
Work:	Fax:
E-mail:	
Birthday:	
Notes:	

Name:

Address:	
Home:	Cell:
Work:	Fax:
E-mail:	
Birthday:	
Notes:	

Name:

Address:	
Home:	Cell:
Work:	Fax:
E-mail:	
Birthday:	
Notes:	

Name:	
Address:	
Home:	Cell:
Work:	Fax:
E-mail:	
Birthday:	
Notes:	

Name:	
Address:	
Home:	Cell:
Work:	Fax:
E-mail:	
Birthday:	
Notes:	

Name:	
Address:	
Home:	Cell:
Work:	Fax:
E-mail:	
Birthday:	
Notes:	

Name:	
Address:	
Home:	Cell:
Work:	Fax:
E-mail:	
Birthday:	
Notes:	

Name:	
Address:	
Home:	Cell:
Work:	Fax:
E-mail:	
Birthday:	
Notes:	

T

Name:	
Address:	
Home:	Cell:
Work:	Fax:
E-mail:	
Birthday:	
Notes:	

Name:	
Address:	
Home:	Cell:
Work:	Fax:
E-mail:	
Birthday:	
Notes:	

Name:	
Address:	
Home:	Cell:
Work:	Fax:
E-mail:	
Birthday:	
Notes:	

T

Name:	
Address:	
Home:	Cell:
Work:	Fax:
E-mail:	
Birthday:	
Notes:	

Name:	
Address:	
Home:	Cell:
Work:	Fax:
E-mail:	
Birthday:	
Notes:	

Name:	
Address:	
Home:	Cell:
Work:	Fax:
E-mail:	
Birthday:	
Notes:	

Name:	
Address:	
Home:	Cell:
Work:	Fax:
E-mail:	
Birthday:	
Notes:	

Name:

Address:

Home:	Cell:
Work:	Fax:

E-mail:

Birthday:

Notes:

Name:

Address:

Home:	Cell:
Work:	Fax:

E-mail:

Birthday:

Notes:

Name:

Address:

Home:	Cell:
Work:	Fax:

E-mail:

Birthday:

Notes:

U

Name:	
Address:	
Home:	Cell:
Work:	Fax:
E-mail:	
Birthday:	
Notes:	

Name:	
Address:	
Home:	Cell:
Work:	Fax:
E-mail:	
Birthday:	
Notes:	

Name:	
Address:	
Home:	Cell:
Work:	Fax:
E-mail:	
Birthday:	
Notes:	

Name:

Address:

Home: Cell:

Work: Fax:

E-mail:

Birthday:

Notes:

Name:

Address:

Home: Cell:

Work: Fax:

E-mail:

Birthday:

Notes:

Name:

U

Address:

Home: Cell:

Work: Fax:

E-mail:

Birthday:

Notes:

Name:	
Address:	
Home:	Cell:
Work:	Fax:
E-mail:	
Birthday:	
Notes:	

Name:	
Address:	
Home:	Cell:
Work:	Fax:
E-mail:	
Birthday:	
Notes:	

Name:	
Address:	
Home:	Cell:
Work:	Fax:
E-mail:	
Birthday:	
Notes:	

Name:

Address:

Home: Cell:

Work: Fax:

E-mail:

Birthday:

Notes:

Name:

Address:

Home: Cell:

Work: Fax:

E-mail:

Birthday:

Notes:

Name:

Address:

Home: Cell:

Work: Fax:

E-mail:

Birthday:

Notes:

U

Name:	
Address:	
Home:	Cell:
Work:	Fax:
E-mail:	
Birthday:	
Notes:	

Name:	
Address:	
Home:	Cell:
Work:	Fax:
E-mail:	
Birthday:	
Notes:	

Name:	
Address:	
Home:	Cell:
Work:	Fax:
E-mail:	
Birthday:	
Notes:	

V

Name:	
Address:	
Home:	Cell:
Work:	Fax:
E-mail:	
Birthday:	
Notes:	

Name:	
Address:	
Home:	Cell:
Work:	Fax:
E-mail:	
Birthday:	
Notes:	

Name:	
Address:	
Home:	Cell:
Work:	Fax:
E-mail:	
Birthday:	
Notes:	

V

Name:

Address:

Home: Cell:

Work: Fax:

E-mail:

Birthday:

Notes:

Name:

Address:

Home: Cell:

Work: Fax:

E-mail:

Birthday:

Notes:

V

Name:

Address:

Home: Cell:

Work: Fax:

E-mail:

Birthday:

Notes:

Name:

Address:

Home:	Cell:
Work:	Fax:

E-mail:

Birthday:

Notes:

Name:

Address:

Home:	Cell:
Work:	Fax:

E-mail:

Birthday:

Notes:

Name:

Address:

Home:	Cell:
Work:	Fax:

E-mail:

Birthday:

Notes:

V

Name:
Address:
Home: Cell:
Work: Fax:
E-mail:
Birthday:
Notes:

Name:
Address:
Home: Cell:
Work: Fax:
E-mail:
Birthday:
Notes:

V

Name:
Address:
Home: Cell:
Work: Fax:
E-mail:
Birthday:
Notes:

Name:

Address:

Home: Cell:

Work: Fax:

E-mail:

Birthday:

Notes:

Name:

Address:

Home: Cell:

Work: Fax:

E-mail:

Birthday:

Notes:

Name:

Address:

Home: Cell:

Work: Fax:

E-mail:

Birthday:

Notes:

Name:

Address:

Home: Cell:

Work: Fax:

E-mail:

Birthday:

Notes:

Name:

Address:

Home: Cell:

Work: Fax:

E-mail:

Birthday:

Notes:

Name:

Address:

Home: Cell:

Work: Fax:

E-mail:

Birthday:

Notes:

W

Name:

Address:

| Home: | Cell: |
| Work: | Fax: |

E-mail:

Birthday:

Notes:

Name:

Address:

| Home: | Cell: |
| Work: | Fax: |

E-mail:

Birthday:

Notes:

Name:

Address:

| Home: | Cell: |
| Work: | Fax: |

E-mail:

Birthday:

Notes:

W

Name:	
Address:	
Home:	Cell:
Work:	Fax:
E-mail:	
Birthday:	
Notes:	

Name:	
Address:	
Home:	Cell:
Work:	Fax:
E-mail:	
Birthday:	
Notes:	

Name:	
Address:	
Home:	Cell:
Work:	Fax:
E-mail:	
Birthday:	
Notes:	

W

Name:

Address:

| Home: | Cell: |
| Work: | Fax: |

E-mail:

Birthday:

Notes:

Name:

Address:

| Home: | Cell: |
| Work: | Fax: |

E-mail:

Birthday:

Notes:

Name:

Address:

| Home: | Cell: |
| Work: | Fax: |

E-mail:

Birthday:

Notes:

W

Name:	
Address:	
Home:	Cell:
Work:	Fax:
E-mail:	
Birthday:	
Notes:	

Name:	
Address:	
Home:	Cell:
Work:	Fax:
E-mail:	
Birthday:	
Notes:	
•	

Name:	
Address:	
Home:	Cell:
Work:	Fax:
E-mail:	
Birthday:	
Notes:	

W

Name:	
Address:	
Home:	Cell:
Work:	Fax:
E-mail:	
Birthday:	
Notes:	

Name:	
Address:	
Home:	Cell:
Work:	Fax:
E-mail:	
Birthday:	
Notes:	

Name:	
Address:	
Home:	Cell:
Work:	Fax:
E-mail:	
Birthday:	
Notes:	

W

Name:	
Address:	
Home:	Cell:
Work:	Fax:
E-mail:	
Birthday:	
Notes:	

Name:	
Address:	
Home:	Cell:
Work:	Fax:
E-mail:	
Birthday:	
Notes:	

Name:	
Address:	
Home:	Cell:
Work:	Fax:
E-mail:	
Birthday:	
Notes:	

X

Name:	
Address:	
Home:	Cell:
Work:	Fax:
E-mail:	
Birthday:	
Notes:	

Name:	
Address:	
Home:	Cell:
Work:	Fax:
E-mail:	
Birthday:	
Notes:	

Name:	
Address:	
Home:	Cell:
Work:	Fax:
E-mail:	
Birthday:	
Notes:	

X

Name:

Address:

Home: Cell:

Work: Fax:

E-mail:

Birthday:

Notes:

Name:

Address:

Home: Cell:

Work: Fax:

E-mail:

Birthday:

Notes:

Name:

Address:

Home: Cell:

X

Work: Fax:

E-mail:

Birthday:

Notes:

Name:

Address:

Home: Cell:

Work: Fax:

E-mail:

Birthday:

Notes:

Name:

Address:

Home: Cell:

Work: Fax:

E-mail:

Birthday:

Notes:

Name:

Address:

Home: Cell:

Work: Fax:

E-mail:

Birthday:

Notes:

X

Name:

Address:

Home:	Cell:
Work:	Fax:

E-mail:

Birthday:

Notes:

Name:

Address:

Home:	Cell:
Work:	Fax:

E-mail:

Birthday:

Notes:

Name:

Address:

Home:	Cell:
Work:	Fax:

E-mail:

Birthday:

Notes:

Name:	
Address:	
Home:	Cell:
Work:	Fax:
E-mail:	
Birthday:	
Notes:	

Name:	
Address:	
Home:	Cell:
Work:	Fax:
E-mail:	
Birthday:	
Notes:	

Name:	
Address:	
Home:	Cell:
Work:	Fax:
E-mail:	
Birthday:	
Notes:	

X

Name:	
Address:	
Home:	Cell:
Work:	Fax:
E-mail:	
Birthday:	
Notes:	

Name:	
Address:	
Home:	Cell:
Work:	Fax:
E-mail:	
Birthday:	
Notes:	

Name:	
Address:	
Home:	Cell:
Work:	Fax:
E-mail:	
Birthday:	
Notes:	

Y

Name:	
Address:	
Home:	Cell:
Work:	Fax:
E-mail:	
Birthday:	
Notes:	

Name:	
Address:	
Home:	Cell:
Work:	Fax:
E-mail:	
Birthday:	
Notes:	

Name:	
Address:	
Home:	Cell:
Work:	Fax:
E-mail:	
Birthday:	
Notes:	

Name:

Address:

Home:	Cell:
Work:	Fax:

E-mail:

Birthday:

Notes:

Name:

Address:

Home:	Cell:
Work:	Fax:

E-mail:

Birthday:

Notes:

Name:

Address:

Home:	Cell:
Work:	Fax:

E-mail:

Birthday:

Notes:

Y

Name:	
Address:	
Home:	Cell:
Work:	Fax:
E-mail:	
Birthday:	
Notes:	

Name:	
Address:	
Home:	Cell:
Work:	Fax:
E-mail:	
Birthday:	
Notes:	

Name:	
Address:	
Home:	Cell:
Work:	Fax:
E-mail:	
Birthday:	
Notes:	

Y

Name:	
Address:	
Home:	Cell:
Work:	Fax:
E-mail:	
Birthday:	
Notes:	

Name:	
Address:	
Home:	Cell:
Work:	Fax:
E-mail:	
Birthday:	
Notes:	

Name:	
Address:	
Home:	Cell:
Work:	Fax:
E-mail:	
Birthday:	
Notes:	

Y

Name:	
Address:	
Home:	Cell:
Work:	Fax:
E-mail:	
Birthday:	
Notes:	

Name:	
Address:	
Home:	Cell:
Work:	Fax:
E-mail:	
Birthday:	
Notes:	

Name:	
Address:	
Home:	Cell:
Work:	Fax:
E-mail:	
Birthday:	
Notes:	

Y

Name:

Address:

Home: Cell:

Work: Fax:

E-mail:

Birthday:

Notes:

Name:

Address:

Home: Cell:

Work: Fax:

E-mail:

Birthday:

Notes:

Name:

Address:

Home: Cell:

Work: Fax:

E-mail:

Birthday:

Notes:

Z

Name:	
Address:	
Home:	Cell:
Work:	Fax:
E-mail:	
Birthday:	
Notes:	

Name:	
Address:	
Home:	Cell:
Work:	Fax:
E-mail:	
Birthday:	
Notes:	

Name:	
Address:	
Home:	Cell:
Work:	Fax:
E-mail:	
Birthday:	
Notes:	

Z

Name:	
Address:	
Home:	Cell:
Work:	Fax:
E-mail:	
Birthday:	
Notes:	

Name:	
Address:	
Home:	Cell:
Work:	Fax:
E-mail:	
Birthday:	
Notes:	

Name:	
Address:	
Home:	Cell:
Work:	Fax:
E-mail:	
Birthday:	
Notes:	

Z

Name:	
Address:	
Home:	Cell:
Work:	Fax:
E-mail:	
Birthday:	
Notes:	

Name:	
Address:	
Home:	Cell:
Work:	Fax:
E-mail:	
Birthday:	
Notes:	

Name:	
Address:	
Home:	Cell:
Work:	Fax:
E-mail:	
Birthday:	
Notes:	

Z

Name:

Address:

Home: Cell:

Work: Fax:

E-mail:

Birthday:

Notes:

Name:

Address:

Home: Cell:

Work: Fax:

E-mail:

Birthday:

Notes:

Name:

Address:

Home: Cell:

Work: Fax:

E-mail:

Birthday:

Notes:

Z

Name:	
Address:	
Home:	Cell:
Work:	Fax:
E-mail:	
Birthday:	
Notes:	

Name:	
Address:	
Home:	Cell:
Work:	Fax:
E-mail:	
Birthday:	
Notes:	

Name:	
Address:	
Home:	Cell:
Work:	Fax:
E-mail:	
Birthday:	
Notes:	

Z

Notes

Notes

Thank you for choosing

Address Book

by I. S. Anderson

Other Titles by I. S. Anderson

5-Year Journal

A5 Dotted Notebook

Change Your Life Guided Journal

Food & Fitness Journal

Food Journal and Blood Sugar Log

**Health Journal: Discover Food Intolerances
and Allergies**

Password Log

Workout Journal: Interval Training

For inquiries or to provide feedback, contact:
nahjpress@outlook.com

Made in the USA
Columbia, SC
27 May 2017